Americanah

by Chimamanda Ngozi
Adichie

BOOK ANALYSIS

By Maria Aalto

Americanah

by Chimamanda Ngozi Adichie

CHIMAMANDA NGOZI ADICHIE

NIGERIAN WRITER

- **Born in Enugu (Nigeria) in 1977.**
- **Notable works:**
  - *Purple Hibiscus* (2003), novel
  - *Half of a Yellow Sun* (2006), novel
  - *We Should All Be Feminists* (2014), essay

Chimamanda Ngozi Adichie is a widely read Nigerian author and a feminist icon.

Adichie grew up in Nsukka, Nigeria. She completed her studies in the United States, and she now divides her time between the two countries.

Adichie's work has been translated into over 30 languages. She has received various awards for her novels, including the Commonwealth Writers' Prize: Best First Book for *Purple Hibiscus* and the National Book Critics Circle Award for *Americanah*. She is also a writer of short stories and non-fiction. Her TED talks *The Danger of a*

Single Story (2009) and *We Should All Be Feminists* (2012) have been widely viewed and commented upon. The latter, which has been published as a book, has sparked a conversation about feminism. Indeed, feminism and the exploration of gender roles are also important parts of Adichie's fiction. Other themes present in her writing include race, religion, love and Nigerian culture and history.

AMERICANAH

A LOVE STORY AND A SOCIALLY CONSCIOUS NOVEL ABOUT RACE

- **Genre:** novel
- **Reference edition:** Adichie, C. N. (2014) *Americanah*. New York: Anchor Books.
- **1st edition:** 2013
- **Themes:** love, race, immigration, home, gender, beauty

Americanah is a multifaceted novel which tackles various social issues, including race, gender and immigration. Ifemelu, the novel's protagonist, is a Nigerian who discovers a new identity, namely being black, in the United States. She shares her observations in the form of an anonymous blog about race. Adichie explores what it means to be black, a woman and an immigrant, among other things, through Ifemelu's (and other characters') experiences. The novel highlights differences between distinct marginalised groups, such as African immigrants and African-Americans, as well as the solidarity that exits between distinct groups.

As well as being a socially conscious novel, *Americanah* is also a love story. Ifemelu and Obinze, the boyfriend from her youth, share a bond so strong that years spent on different continents with virtually no contact with each other, and other relationships they have had since their separation, cannot undo the love they share.

SUMMARY

LEAVING THE UNITED STATES

Americanah is the story of two Nigerians, Ifemelu and Obinze. The novel begins with Ifemelu, who is about to leave the United States and go back to her home country, Nigeria, observing the environment she is preparing to leave behind. She has closed her successful blog about race as she prepares to begin her new life back home but keeps observing the people around her as she if she were collecting ideas for her blog. She goes to get her hair braided in an African hair salon and observes the women in the salon, and thinks about her life now, and back in Nigeria. Her thoughts drift to Obinze, her first love. She knows Obinze has become a successful business-man, is married and has a little daughter. Ifemelu and Obinze have had very little contact with each other since their relationship broke down, but they have thought of each other often.

GROWING UP IN NIGERIA

The narrative moves to describe Ifemelu's youth in Nigeria. Her memories focus on important people in her life: her friends, her parents, Aunty Uju, who is the family member Ifemelu feels closest to, and, of course, Obinze. Ifemelu and Obinze meet at school and fall in love at a friend's party. Their relationship is close and honest from the beginning. Ifemelu and Obinze feel that they understand each other and share a deep emotional bond. They also share common interests, such as reading books, although their tastes are not always the same. Obinze is particularly interested in American culture and literature, and dreams of living in the United States. After they finish school, Ifemelu and Obinze start studying at the University of Nsukka in Nigeria. Later, because their courses are disrupted by strikes, Ifemelu applies for, and succeeds in obtaining, a partial scholarship to study in America. She starts to prepare for her departure. She and Obinze agree that he will join her in America when he graduates.

IFEMELU'S AMERICAN EXPERIENCE

Ifemelu arrives in America and first spends the summer in Brooklyn with Aunty Uju, who has already been living in America for some years. She helps her aunt look after her cousin Dike, with whom Ifemelu becomes close. In the autumn Ifemelu starts studying in Philadelphia. She is initially excited to be in America, but she struggles to adapt to the local culture. Moreover, she cannot find work and worries about not being able to pay her rent. In desperation, she accepts an encounter of sexual nature (though no intercourse takes place) for a hundred dollars with a man she had initially contacted for a personal assistant position. After this Ifemelu becomes depressed and cuts contact with Obinze.

Ifemelu's friend Ginika helps her find work as a babysitter for a wealthy family. This ends her financial worries, and she starts to adapt better to life in the United States. Ifemelu begins a relationship with the cousin of her employer, Curt. She is happy with him, but as he is a wealthy white man, his background is very different from hers. Because of this, they do not always understand one another, but they learn from each other. Curt helps Ifemelu find work that allows her to receive her green card. They stay together for several years, but finally the relationship ends with Ifemelu's infidelity. Soon after that, Ifemelu starts to write a blog on race in America, as observed by a non-American black woman. Her blog becomes very successful, which allows her financial freedom and a way to observe the identity of being black, an identity which she discovered in America.

Ifemelu begins a new relationship, this time with an African-American professor, Blaine. She moves to New Haven to be with him. While Ifemelu and Blaine have the shared experience of being privileged, educated black individuals in America, they are also very different because of their dissimilar cultural backgrounds. She is happy with her life in America with Blaine but eventually feels the urge to go back home. Neither one of Ifemelu's relationships in America were as close and as passionate as her relationship with Obinze.

OBINZE'S BRITISH EXPERIENCE

Obinze cannot fulfil his dream of living in America because his visa application is rejected in the post-9/11 circumstances. He moves to London instead. His visa expires, and he lives as an undocumented immigrant in England. His life in London is very different from what he is used to as a young man from an educated, middle-class background. He works odd jobs under someone else's name and plans a sham wedding which would allow him to stay in England. However, when he is about to marry, he gets arrested and eventually deported back to Nigeria. Back in Nigeria Obinze becomes a successful business-man and marries a beautiful woman, but he does not feel entirely content with his new life.

RECONNECTING WITH NIGERIA AND OBINZE

Ifemelu's plans to return home are delayed by Dike's attempted suicide. Ifemelu rushes to be with her beloved cousin, who is now a teenager. Dike starts to recover and urges Ifemelu to go back home as she had planned. Later, Dike comes to visit his cousin in Nigeria. Upon her arrival in Lagos, Ifemelu finds both herself and Nigeria changed, but she eventually finds her place in her home country. She initially works at a women's magazine, but finally quits her job and starts blogging again. This time, however, she writes on various subjects relevant to life in Lagos, as a blog about race would not work in Nigeria. Ifemelu has become a confident, independent woman who does not want to let her relationships or her employer define her. Ifemelu and Obinze reconnect and discover that they still love each other. After struggling with his sense of responsibility towards his family, Obinze leaves his wife to be with Ifemelu.

CHARACTER STUDY

IFEMELU

Ifemelu is a Nigerian woman from Lagos. She moves to the United States to pursue her studies, and spends 13 years there before finally returning to Lagos. She is an independent, outspoken, intelligent woman who spends a great deal of her time observing the people around her. In America Ifemelu makes an interesting discovery: she is black. In Nigeria the colour of her skin was not an important part of her identity, as in her home country she is defined by her ethnicity and gender rather than race. In America, it seems that before being Igbo (her ethnic group in Nigeria) or even Nigerian, she is black. Ifemelu makes sense of this experience by writing a blog on race in America, as observed by a non-American black woman. She discovers that while there are many cultural differences between Africans and African-Americans, there is a shared experience of being marginalised, which calls for solidarity between black people, and understanding from white people. Ifemelu's experiences regarding race can be observed through her romantic relationships. Ifemelu has three important relationships. Her first love, Obinze, is also Nigerian and Igbo. He is the love of her life, as she is his, although they both have other meaningful relationships. Her second major relationship is with Curt, who is American and white. He is the partner who is the most different from Ifemelu, but they have a loving relationship which lasts for several years. Ifemelu's third relationship is with Blaine, an African-American man, who, obviously, is black like her, but from a different culture. These relationships and the other social interactions Ifemelu experiences change her and inspire her to reflect on her situation. She explores what it means to be black, Nigerian, an immigrant, middle-class, a woman and someone who has returned to her home country after living abroad for several years.

OBINZE

Obinze is a calm, kind and intelligent Nigerian man. He is well educated and has grown up in a middle-class environment. He has a close relationship with his mother, who is a university professor. Probably at least in part because of this, Obinze is always respectful towards women. Obinze and Ifemelu share a deep emotional bond which is not broken by years spent apart with virtually no contact with one another. As a boy and a young man, Obinze dreams of living in America, but he is not able to fulfil his dreams because he is unable to obtain a visa for the United States. He moves to England on a six-month research assistant visa. After his visa expires he lives a marginalised life as an undocumented immigrant, and he is eventually deported back to Nigeria, where he becomes a successful businessman. Obinze becomes disenchanted, more reserved and less optimistic as a result of his experiences, but at the core he remains the same kind and intelligent person he always was. When Ifemelu returns to Nigeria, she discovers that he is still the same man she fell in love with in her youth.

CURT

Curt is a privileged, wealthy, white American man. He is kind and handsome, and always ready to charm those around him. Curt is not always aware of the racial issues present in his society because he has never experienced them personally, but he is willing to learn. He represents a white person who can be blind to racism because of his lack of understanding and experience, but who also can be useful for the black community cause because of his empathy and willingness to listen to other people's experiences. As a person with power, he can yield this power in favour of those who are marginalised if he is made aware of the issues. Ifemelu learns about American culture from Curt, and Curt learns about African culture and the experience of being black in America from Ifemelu. Still, sometimes Curt seems unable to fully understand Ifemelu, and she is sometimes irritated by this. Curt and Ifemelu spend several happy years together, and although Ifemelu has never felt the same sense of belonging together with Curt as she did with Obinze, she was able to imagine a future with him at one point. Ifemelu continues to value him after the end of their relationship, and even calls him to catch up years later when she is back in Nigeria.

BLAINE

Blaine is an African-American professor of political science at Yale. He is an intellectual and a man who is deeply driven by his ethical principles. Ifemelu admires these qualities in him, but sometimes she finds that their cultural differences make them look at the world in different ways. For example, when a white woman asks to touch Ifemelu's afro, Blaine thinks she should be offended by the woman's request, but Ifemelu does not see it as a problem. She thinks that he "expected her to feel what she did not know how to feel" (p. 388). Despite their cultural differences, Ifemelu and Blaine have a lot in common. Most importantly, they are both intelligent people actively exploring what it means to be black in America (and in the rest of the world). They are united in their excitement about Barack Obama's presidential campaign, which is a major victory for black people in America. Although Ifemelu has a deep and meaningful relationship with Blaine, it does not compare to the bond she shared with Obinze, nor is it enough to keep her from moving back to Nigeria.

AUNTY UJU

Aunty Uju is an intelligent, hardworking woman. Her weak point is that she gets involved with men who do not treat her well. She is Ifemelu's father's sister (or the family calls her his sister, although she is, in fact, his cousin). Aunty Uju is the family member Ifemelu feels closest to. Growing up, Ifemelu looked up to her and asked her for advice. As an adult, Ifemelu's relationship with Aunty Uju transforms into a relationship between equals. Ifemelu struggles to understand Uju's relationships with men who are beneath her, but she continues to support her aunt even when she does not agree with the choices she makes. In Nigeria, Uju is a military general's mistress. After the general dies, she moves to America with their son Dike, who is a toddler at the time. After initial struggles, Uju, who is a doctor, passes her exams so that she can practice medicine in the United States. Her struggles are representative of the diverse problems African immigrants and black women face in America, such as prejudice from white patients when working as a doctor. Aunty Uju and Dike represent Ifemelu's family in America.

DIKE

Dike is Ifemelu's cousin. Dike and Ifemelu form a close relationship when Ifemelu spends her first summer in America babysitting him. Dike admires Ifemelu and seeks her guidance. He represents a child of an African immigrant, torn between two cultures. He grows up in an African household but is surrounded by American culture. Dike's experiences explore the racial dynamics in America from a child's perspective. After his mother starts to practice medicine, they move to a predominantly white neighbourhood, which forces Dike to explore his identity as 'the black kid'. Dike's motives for his attempted suicide are not fully explained, but it is a deep shock to his mother and his cousin. Ifemelu drops everything to be with Dike, but he eventually tells her to go ahead with her plans to move back to Nigeria. Dike visits Ifemelu in Nigeria and remains an important person in her life even after they no longer live in the same country.

ANALYSIS

A POSTCOLONIAL NOVEL

Americanah can be described as a postcolonial novel. In its broadest definition, the term postcolonial refers to "all the cultures affected by the imperial process from the moment of colonization to present day" (Ashcroft et al., 1989: 2). While other more restrictive definitions exist, this broad definition is useful because it encompasses the full scale of cultures and literature that fit under the term. This is relevant to *Americanah*, because it deals with two very dissimilar kinds of postcolonial societies. What is especially important to keep in mind when analysing *Americanah* is that Nigeria is a country with numerous ethnic groups *native to Africa.* The United States, on the other hand, is a predominantly white society, and thus largely representative of the former colonial power (while not all white Americans are descendants of the colonialists, they belong to the historically dominant race). Only a very small part of the current population are native

Americans, and the history of the black minority in the United States is marked by slavery and segregation. Independence from the colonial power thus meant different things for the two countries. Both countries suffered from the colonial domination, but because of these and other differences, they have evolved in distinct directions.

Terms relevant to both postcolonial societies present in *Americanah* are 'the other' and 'othering'. This means dividing people into 'us' and 'them', often meaning the white Western people and the non-white other. This is at the heart of colonial discourse which describes the colonized people as 'primitive' and 'inferior'. The problem with this binary distinction is that it fails to account for other ways of 'othering' such as discrimination based on gender, social class, sexuality and disability (Ramone, 2011: 110). Furthermore, the simple distinction between white and non-white people is not adequate to describe the different cultures, individuals and power dynamics within and across both of these groups. Nevertheless, othering based on race is a real issue in the United States and around the world, and these dynamics, along with other forms of othering, are explored in detail in the novel. The presence of various types of characters with distinct backgrounds, experiences and opinions provides a nuanced and multifaceted investigation of the themes, but without losing sight of the gravity of issues such as racism.

The most important themes connected to othering present in *Americanah* are race, immigration and gender.

RACE

The most obvious theme in *Americanah* is race. Ifemelu, who grew up in Nigeria, had not thought much about race before arriving in America. Race became a part of her identity only after she discovered its significance in America. She writes in her blog, addressing non-American black people in America: "when you make the choice to come to America, you become black. Stop arguing. Stop saying I'm Jamaican or I'm Ghanaian. America doesn't care" (p. 273). This shows not only that race matters in the United States, but also that other markers of one's identity, such as nationality, are not given as much importance in America. Ifemelu's perspective is interesting because she explores race relations both as an outsider, as a foreigner, and as an insider, as a black person in the United States.

 The fact that there are black characters with diverse cultural backgrounds in the novel is interesting. This can be observed, for example, in the two separate student unions at Ifemelu's university: the African Students Association, attended mainly by African students, and the Black Student Union, attended mainly by African-American students (p. 172). Moreover, Ifemelu and her African-American boyfriend, Blaine, do not always see the world in the same way, as can be observed in the episode where the white woman touches Ifemelu's hair (see 'Character Study' section). However, the shared experience of being othered as black people calls for solidarity between different kinds of people wanting to fight racial inequality. Furthermore, Ifemelu shows that if one is aware of the sociohistorical facts which contribute to the current social reality and to diverse people's sense of identity, one can approach people with different views with greater empathy. This can be observed from how Ifemelu answers Laura, her employer's sister, when she says that a Ugandan woman she knew did not have "all those issues" (p. 207) that another, African-American woman had: "Maybe when the African American's father was not allowed to vote because he was black, the Ugandan's father was running for parliament or studying at Oxford" (*ibid*.). For more information on solidarity between African and African-American people in *Americanah*, see McCoy (2017).

IMMIGRATION

Immigration is another important theme in *Americanah*. The immigrant experience can be observed through the experiences of characters like Ifemelu, Obinze, Aunty Uju and Dike. Ifemelu is a Nigerian immigrant in the United States. She comes to America as a student. Her family is not wealthy, but she is not fleeing hunger or persecution in her home country. This is true also for Obinze. In fact, these characters tell an immigration story which is different from the one that often is portrayed in the Western media: Obinze and Ifemelu are educated young people from middle-class backgrounds (even if Ifemelu's family is less wealthy than Obinze's, she is not poor). They are merely hungry for choice and certainty, and curious about discovering other countries and cultures. Obinze, who lives in England as an undocumented immigrant, wonders if the people who understand the desperation of people fleeing wars, hunger and disasters would understand his circumstances (p. 341).

Ifemelu, Uju and Obinze must learn to adapt to new cultures and deal with financial, administrative and social problems resulting from their immigrant status. Dike's situation is different. He is the child of an immigrant, but he grows up in America. He has no memories of Nigeria, but his family is Nigerian. He is torn between two cultures, and attempts to find his place in the world and build his identity based on two cultures. Living abroad also changes the identities of those who move to other countries later in life. The title of the book, *Americanah*, refers to a Nigerian who returns from America radically changed. When Ifemelu leaves for America, her friends tease her by saying that when she returns from America, she will be a "serious Americanah" (p. 123). In fact, when Ifemelu does return to Nigeria, her tastes, ideas and interests have changed. Ifemelu does not want to be an 'Americanah', but she must admit that years spent away have left their mark on her. This is another side of immigration: after spending a significant period of time abroad a person must re-evaluate their sense of identity and their ideas about home.

GENDER

Gender is another important aspect in this novel. Ifemelu is a strong, independent, outspoken woman. Although her romantic relationships form an important part of the novel, she is not defined by the men in her life. She is affected by her relationships, but she makes her own decisions. In America, Ifemelu becomes aware of race. In Nigeria, on the other hand, she seems more aware of gender issues. She does not like the fact that her Nigerian friends hold marriage as their main goal. She does not have anything against marriage and relationships, but she does not like the way women are expected to aspire to marriage in way that is not expected of men. In her essay on feminism, Adichie explains that a well-meaning journalist had advised her not to call herself a feminist, because "feminists are women who are unhappy because they cannot find husbands" (Adichie, 2014: 9). Ifemelu, who is independent and refuses marriage as a goal in itself can be described as a feminist. The fact that she has healthy loving relationships with men shows the absurdity of the journalist's statement. Feminism and love stories can go hand in hand, as long as the man and the woman are equals in the relationship and are equally invested in it.

A LOVE STORY

Despite having a strong female protagonist who does not have to marry a man to succeed in life, *Americanah* is a love story. The bond between Ifemelu and Obinze is one of the most remarkable aspects of the novel. Their touching love story reaches something universally human which crosses boundaries of race, gender and country of origin. While readers from different cultures might interpret some choices, such as divorce, differently, understanding the meaning of the bond that forms between two people who love each other is universal.

STYLE

Three important elements regarding the novel's style are the fact that it is a third person narrative focused on Ifemelu's and Obinze's experiences, the use of Ifemelu's blog entries to discuss ideas and the use of the Igbo language.

Regarding the style and language used in *Americanah*, most of the novel is written as a third person narrative. The narration focuses on two points of view: many parts of the book are told focusing on Ifemelu's experiences, and some parts are told from Obinze's perspective. This allows the reader to observe the story as it is lived by these two characters. In addition, the narration includes another technique: some of Ifemelu's blog entries are included in the novel, which permits a deep exploration of ideas. It would be hard to explain many complex ideas about race in form of dialogue, because one of the characters would have to deliver long speeches, which would need special circumstances to be believable. The blog entries do this naturally. Another interesting aspect regarding style in *Americanah* is the use of the Igbo language, which brings the Nigerian characters to life and functions as a marker of their identity. The style of the novel functions to support themes discussed above.

FURTHER REFLECTION

SOME QUESTIONS TO THINK ABOUT...

- Ifemelu decides to stop conforming to Western beauty standards by stopping straightening her hair. Discuss the political implications of her decision.
- Ifemelu's blog about race is anonymous. How do you think this impacts the way in which she can express herself?
- Ifemelu first learns to speak English with an American accent, but then decides to switch back to her Nigerian accent. Discuss the meaning of this choice with regard to her cultural identity.
- What do you think is the impact of the use of the Igbo language in the novel?
- Discuss the most important differences between Nigerian culture and African-American culture in the novel.
- Why is race experienced so differently by black Americans and black Africans? How does

Ifemelu's blog help you understand these dynamics?

- Discuss Ifemelu's romantic relationships. What does she learn from each of her partners?
- In your opinion, why did Obinze stay in England after his visa expired? He cites his hunger for "choice and certainty" (p. 341) as his motivation. Discuss his reasoning and his uncertainty regarding Western people's ability to understand him and others like him.
- Discuss the title of the book. Has Ifemelu become an 'Americanah'? What is the significance of the changes she goes through in relation to her home country?

We want to hear from you!
Leave a comment on your online library
and share your favourite books on social media!

FURTHER READING

REFERENCE EDITION

- Adichie, C. N. (2014) *Americanah*. New York: Anchor Books.

REFERENCE STUDIES

- Adichie, C. N. (2014) *We Should All Be Feminists*. London: Fourth Estate.

- Ashcroft et al. (1989) *The Empire writes back: theory and practice in post-colonial literatures*. London: Routledge.

- McCoy, S. A. (2017) The "Outsider Within": counter-narratives of the "New" African diaspora in Chimamanda Ngozi Adichie's Americanah (2013). *Journal of the African Literature Association*. 11:3, pp. 279-294.

- Ramone, J. (2011) *Postcolonial Theories*. London: Palgrave Macmillan.

- Tunca, D. (No date) *The Chimamanda Ngozi Adichie Website*. [Online] [Accessed 23 September 2018]. Available from: <http://www.cerep.ulg.ac.be/adichie/index.html>

ADDITIONAL SOURCES

- Official author website: https://www.chima-manda.com/
  Readers of Americanah might find the section titled "Ifemelu's blog" particularly interesting.

MORE FROM BRIGHTSUMMARIES.COM

- Reading guide – *Half of a Yellow Sun* by Chimanada Ngozi Adichie.

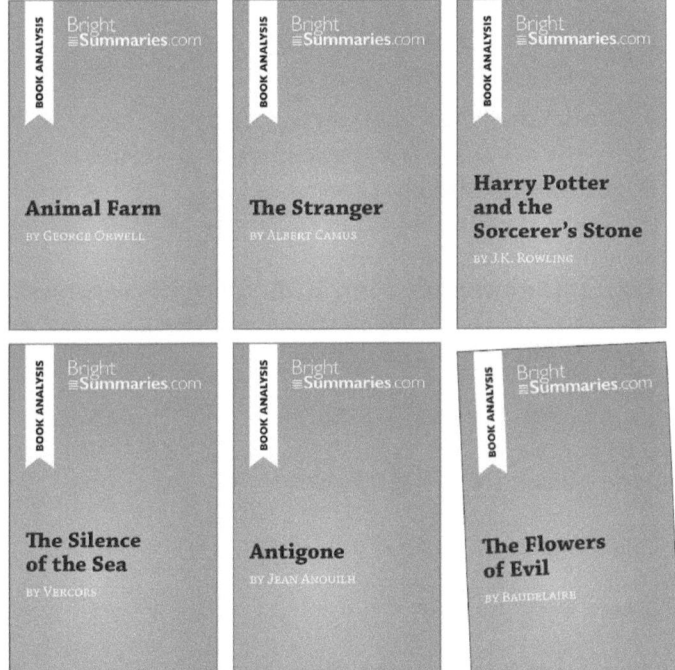

www.brightsummaries.com

Ebook EAN: 9782808012454

Paperback EAN: 9782808012461

Legal Deposit: D/2018/12603/378

Cover: © Primento

Digital conception by Primento, the digital partner of
publishers.